Collins English Library

THE LOVELY LADY
AND OTHER STORIES
D H LAWRENCE

Abridged and simplified by Margery Morris

Illustrations by Maureen and Gordon Gray

HENLEY COLLEGE WITHDRAWN

Contents

Collins: London and Glasgow

© Margery Morris 1981

Published in Great Britain by
William Collins Sons and Co Ltd
Glasgow G4 0NB

Printed by Martin's of Berwick

First published in Collins English Library, 1981

Reprinted 1982, 1984, 1986, 1987, 1988

ISBN 0 00 370129 8

We are grateful to London Weekend Television for
permission to reproduce the photograph which appears on
the cover.
Our thanks are also due to Francesca Annis for granting her
permission.

The Lovely Lady

Pauline Attenborough was seventy-two, but sometimes, in the half-light, she seemed thirty. She really was a wonderful woman. Her clothes were always fashionable, and she had a good figure. She had pretty curved cheeks, a well-shaped nose, and good teeth. Her skin was smooth, and only her eyes showed her age. When she was tired, there were little lines at the corners.

Her niece Cecilia was perhaps the only person in the world who knew that Pauline could make those lines disappear. When Pauline's son Robert came home, her eyes became young and bright and shining. Then she really was a lovely lady; she was a picture painted by Leonardo, a Mona Lisa.

Pauline didn't always look young, of course. She was too clever. When she was with Cecilia, Pauline didn't try. Cecilia, said Pauline, didn't notice things. Cecilia wasn't pretty. Cecilia was thirty; she had no money; and she was in love with Robert. Cecilia didn't matter.

Cecilia, called by her aunt and cousin just 'Ciss', was a big, dark, rather silent young woman. Her father and mother and uncle were all dead. And Aunt Pauline had been in charge of Ciss for five years.

They lived in a very pretty old house, about thirty kilometres from the town. There was a small but pleasant garden.

Robert, who was two years older than Ciss, went to town every day. He was a lawyer. He earned only a hundred pounds a year, and he was secretly ashamed of this. But it didn't matter. Pauline had money. Sometimes she gave him quite a lot, but he always had to thank her for the lovely present.

Like Cecilia, Robert was not good-looking, and he was very silent. He was not very tall, and his face was rather fat. He had grey eyes like his mother, but they were not bright like hers.

may be

Perhaps Ciss was the only person who knew that Robert was shy, and that he always felt he was in the wrong place. But he never did anything about it. He was very interested in the laws of old Mexico, and had a lot of strange old papers about them.

Pauline and Robert had wonderful evenings with these papers. The lovely lady knew a little Spanish. She used to look Spanish, sitting at the table, in her dark brown silk dress, with pearls in her ears, and a high Spanish comb in her hair. In the candle-light – and she placed the candles very carefully – she looked – yes – like a Spanish beauty of thirty-two or three.

Cecilia watched her, and thought she was beautiful. But all the time, in the bottom of her mind, were all the things she knew about her aunt and cousin. And though Robert turned to his mother like a flower in the sun, yet all the time he knew Cecilia was there. He knew that something wasn't quite right. He knew Cecilia was shut out

6

of things.

Every evening after dinner Robert had coffee with his mother and Ciss in the pretty sitting-room. They talked; Pauline was friendly and smiling, and it was very nice. Until there was a little pause. And then Ciss always said goodnight, and took the coffee things out.

And then! Oh, then, the happy talk between mother and son, while they translated the old papers. Pauline was like a girl; Robert seemed older than she was; almost like a teacher with a young pupil. That was how he felt.

Ciss had her own flat, outside the house, over an old coach-house, where Robert kept his car. Ciss had three very nice rooms up there.

But sometimes she did not go to her rooms. In summer, she used to sit on the grass under the sitting-room window. She could hear Pauline's wonderful laugh. And in winter, Ciss used to put on a thick coat, and walk to the end of the garden, and look back at the lighted windows of the room. That room where mother and son were happy together.

Ciss loved Robert, and she believed that Pauline wanted them to marry – after her death. But poor Robert was very shy, shy with men as well as women.

There was a secret, silent feeling between Robert and Ciss, the feeling of two young people who are over-shadowed by the old.

There was another feeling, but Ciss didn't know how to use it. She didn't know how to bring Robert close to her. But she did know that Robert was really a very warm, loving person. And Pauline too knew this! He could not move, could not escape. And he was ashamed that he was not a man.

Sometimes Ciss wanted to say, "Oh Robert, it's all wrong!" But she couldn't.

Aunt Pauline always rested in the afternoon. When the sun shone, she took a sun-bath if possible. There was a little square garden behind the coach-house, with thick bushes all round it. When the sun shone warmly, Ciss used to put a long chair there. There the lovely lady came with her book. Ciss had to stay in her flat, to guard her. Someone might come.

One summer day, Ciss thought she too might take a sun-bath. The roof of the coach-house was flat. So she climbed up there, looked at the sky, and the tree-tops, and the sun, and took off her clothes, and lay down.

It was lovely to lie in the warm sun and air. Some of the cold feeling in her heart seemed to melt away. She had no other lover, but she had the sun! Then suddenly, her heart stood still. She heard a very soft, thoughtful voice, the voice of an old woman; and it seemed to whisper in her ear.

"No, Henry dear! It was not my fault that you died, instead of marrying that Claudia. No, darling. I wanted you to marry her. Though she was not a suitable girl for you."

Ciss was afraid. There must be someone on the roof!

She lifted her head. Nobody! Then there must be someone in the trees. Either that, or – a ghost?

The voice came again.

"No, Henry – no, darling! I told you that you would become tired of her in six months. And it was true, dear, true, true. I only warned you. So when you felt weak, and ill, wanting Claudia and not wanting her – it wasn't my fault. And then you lost courage and went away from me, and died – oh, it was hard for me, hard . . ."

The whispering voice was silent. Cecilia felt cold and afraid. And then she heard it again. Was it a human voice?

"Ah, my heart was wounded. Bleeding! But not broken. I was sad, sad. But it wasn't my fault, dear. And Robert could marry Ciss tomorrow, if he wanted her. But I don't think he cares for marriage."

9

Then Cecilia knew. It was Aunt Pauline's voice. But where was she? She must be lying down there. But was she really speaking? Or had Cecilia heard her thoughts?

Cecilia knew that Pauline had killed her other son, Henry. He was twelve years older than Robert. He died suddenly, when he was twenty-two. He was deeply in love with a young actress. But his mother laughed at him. So he became ill, and died. Because, helpless between his mother and the girl, he could not live.

"I must get up," whispered the voice. "Too much sun is bad."

Cecilia lay on her back, staring at the low wall round the flat roof. She was staring without seeing. There was a hole, a hole in the corner of the wall. Then Cecilia heard the voice again.

"Get up, Pauline. Get up. That's enough for today!"

Cecilia sat up. The voice came from the hole in the wall. There was a pipe there, a rain-water pipe. It went from the roof, down the wall, to the ground. She was not hearing Aunt Pauline's thoughts! Aunt Pauline was talking to herself. And she was worried about Robert.

Aunt Pauline was indeed a strange woman. She had left her husband when Henry was a small child, before Robert was born. She saw her husband sometimes. She even gave him money. Because Pauline had her own money. Her father had lived in the East and in Italy. He had loved beautiful things, and bought them. When he died, Pauline had all his treasures. She went on buying things – paintings, old wooden African figures, things like that, and often she sold them. She

10

made a fortune.

When her husband died she did not marry again. She did not even have any more lovers. Or if she did, no-one knew. No-one knew that Robert was not her husband's child.

Cecilia put on her clothes and picked up her blanket, and went downstairs. As she did, she heard Pauline's call. "All right, Ciss!" Her voice was young again, and rang like a bell.

Cecilia went to take away her aunt's chair. She saw the end of the rain-pipe, in the corner, near the chair. Her aunt had talked into it.

That evening, after coffee, Pauline said, "I'm sleepy. It's all that sun. I'm going to bed. You two stay here and talk." She went out.

Cecilia looked at her cousin. "Would you rather be alone?" she said.

"Oh no," he said. "Do stay."

The windows were open. Robert smoked in a heavy silence. He seemed to carry a weight on his shoulders.

"Do you remember your brother Henry?" said Cecilia suddenly.

He looked up in surprise. "Yes, very well."

"What was he like?"

"Tall, good-looking. Women admired him very much. He was quick and clever, like mother. And very nice, very kind and friendly."

"And did he love your mother?"

"Oh, very much. She loved him too. More than she loved me. I'm not like him at all. I'm dull, and my life is dull."

"And do you mind?"

11

He didn't answer. Her heart sank.

"You see," she said, "my life is dull and empty too. And I mind very much. I want – oh, I want everything!"

His hand was shaking.

"Robert," she said. "Do you like me at all?"

"I like you," he said. His face was white.

"Won't you kiss me? No-one ever kisses me," she said.

He looked at her. He seemed afraid. Then he got up and came over to her and kissed her gently on the cheek.

"What a shame, Ciss," he said softly.

She took his hand.

"And will you sit with me sometimes in the garden?"

He looked at her.

"What about mother?"

Ciss smiled, and looked into his eyes. His face was a painful red.

"I know," he said. "I am no lover of women."

"You don't try," she said.

"Do I have to try?"

"Yes!"

His face was white again. "Perhaps you're right," he said.

After a few minutes, she left him and went to her room.

The weather continued sunny. At night, under the stars, Cecilia sat and waited in silence. She watched the sitting-room window. She saw the lights go out. And she waited. But he did not come. She stayed in the darkness half the night, but she stayed alone.

And then, a few nights later, he did come out.

She rose, and went quickly over the grass to him.

"Don't speak," he said softly.

In silence, in the dark, they walked down the garden and out into a field, and there they stood, under the stars.

"You see," he said. "How can I ask for love, if I don't feel any love in myself?"

"You mean, how can you feel love, when you have no feeling of any kind?"

"Yes. And how can I marry? I've failed. I can't make money, and I can't ask mother for money."

"Then don't think about marriage," she said. "Only love me a little, won't you?"

He gave a short laugh.

"It's difficult to begin," he said.

"Let's sit down," she said. Then, as they sat on the dry grass, she added. "May I touch you? Do you mind?"

"Yes, I do mind. But do as you wish."

He was both shy and honest; but there was murder in his heart.

She touched his black hair with her fingers.

"I suppose I shall turn against mother some day," he said suddenly.

They sat for a while, until it grew cold. Then he held her hand tightly. But he didn't put his arms round her. At last Ciss said goodnight, and went indoors.

The next day, as she lay on the roof taking her sun-bath, and feeling angry, she heard the voice again.

"No, Robert dear. You'll never be like your father. Oh, he was so wonderful. He loved me, he loved me so much." The voice began to speak softly in Italian. Then Cecilia knew that Robert was not the son of Pauline's husband.

The voice continued, "I'm disappointed, Robert. Your father was perfect. But you're like a fish in a tank. And that Ciss is like a cat, fishing for you."

Suddenly Cecilia bent down and put her mouth to the pipe. She said in a deep voice, "Leave Robert alone! Don't kill him too!"

There was dead silence in the hot July afternoon.

Cecilia lay and listened. Her heart was beating hard. At last she heard the whisper.

"Did someone speak?"

Ciss leaned over again.

"Don't kill Robert as you killed me," she said in a deep but small voice.

"Ah! Who is it?" came a sharp little cry.

"Henry!" said the deep voice.

There was dead silence again. At last came the whisper, "I didn't kill Henry. No, no! I loved you, Henry. I only wanted to help you."

"You killed me," said the deep voice. "Now let Robert live. Let him marry!"

Cecilia lay and listened and listened. There was no sound. She put on her clothes and went down to the square garden. Clouds covered the sky and there was thunder in the distance.

"Aunt Pauline!" she called. "Did you hear the thunder?"

"Yes, I'm going in. Don't wait for me," said a weak voice.

The sky grew dark and the storm broke. That night Cecilia dressed for dinner carefully. She

pinned some white flowers on her dress.

Robert was in the sitting room, listening to the rain. Cecilia came in and he watched her with a new look on his face.

The door opened. It was Aunt Pauline. As she came in, Cecilia suddenly put on the light.

Her aunt, in a black dress, stood in the doorway. She looked like an angry old woman.

"Why mother!" said Robert. "You look like a little old lady." He spoke like a child.

"Have you only just discovered that?" she said sharply. "Come down to dinner."

At the table she looked old, very old. Ciss was watching Robert. He was surprised and shocked. He seemed a different man.

His mother ate her food like a hungry animal. As soon as dinner was over she ran upstairs. Robert and Cecilia followed her, silent with surprise.

"I don't want coffee," shouted the old woman. "I'm going. Goodnight." Her voice barked like a dog and she went out, banging the door.

After a while, Robert said, "Mother isn't well. She must see a doctor."

"Yes," said Cecilia.

The evening passed in silence. Robert and Cecilia stayed in the sitting room. They lit a fire. Outside was the cold rain. Each tried to read.

At about ten o'clock the door suddenly opened and Pauline appeared. She went to the fire, and looked at the two young people in hate, real hate.

"You two must get married quickly," she said, "since you are a pair of lovers."

She really was a strange sight. She looked like a piece of lovely Venetian glass, broken into sharp-edged pieces. She left the room again, suddenly.

For a week it went on. Pauline didn't get better. The doctor came and gave her sleeping medicine. She would not look at her son or her niece. When either of them came to her room, she asked, "Well? When's the wedding? Aren't you married yet?"

At first Cecilia was frightened. She understood that her aunt was mad. Nothing like that had ever happened to Pauline before and now, she had

him to kiss her. But he did not, and then the lights went on. After the cinema they went for a walk across the fields. He knew how to make love to a girl. He held her, and kissed her, and his kisses were soft and warm.

So John Thomas became Annie's boy-friend. Some of the other girls were not pleased. But Annie did not mind. She liked John Thomas. When he was near, she felt rich and warm. And he liked her too, more than usual.

But Annie wanted more than a man who kissed her in the dark. She wanted a person, a friend; she wanted to know him better. She did not think he would leave her.

This was a mistake. John Thomas did not want to be more than a man who kissed her in the dark. He didn't like women who wanted to know him better. So he left her.

Annie was very surprised. At first she could not believe it. Then she cried angry tears. She was lonely and unhappy. When he came on the tram-cars and checked the money, he was still smiling. So she decided to have her revenge.

She knew which girls John Thomas had taken out. She went to Nora Purdy. Nora was a tall girl with beautiful yellow hair.

"Who is John Thomas going out with now?" Annie asked.

"I don't know."

"Yes, you do."

"All right, I do. It's not me."

"It's Cissy Meakin, isn't it?"

"Yes."

"Well!" said Annie. "What a man. Who does he think he is? I'd like to push him off the tram."

"Someone will punish him, some day," said Nora.

"They will. I'd like to see it, wouldn't you?"

"I don't mind," said Nora.

But she did mind. She was even more revengeful than Annie.

Annie went round all the girls, and talked to them. Then Cissy Meakin stopped working on the trams. Her mother made her leave. So John Thomas was looking for another girl. He looked at all the girls, and then he saw Annie. "It's safe now," he thought. He liked her.

Annie arranged to walk home with him on Sunday night. She asked him to meet her at 10.15, when the last tram came in.

At the stopping-place the girls had a little waiting-room. It was warm, with a fire. There was a mirror, and tables and chairs, and some tea-things.

All the six girls who knew John Thomas had arranged to work on Sunday afternoon. So, as the cars arrived, they came into the waiting-room. Instead of hurrying home, they sat round the fire, and had a cup of tea.

Outside was the darkness and lawlessness of war-time. John Thomas arrived about a quarter to ten, and put his head round the waiting-room door.

"Is this a meeting?" he asked.

"Yes," said Laura Sharp. "Ladies only."

"Shut the door," said Muriel Baggaley.

"On which side of me?" said John Thomas.

"Come in if you like," said Polly Birkin.

He came in and closed the door behind him. The girls moved to make a place for him at the fire.

22

He took off his heavy coat.

"Any tea?" he said.

Silently, Nora Purdy poured him a cup of tea.

"Want a bit of my bread and butter?" said Muriel Baggaley.

"Yes, give me a bit," he said.

He began to eat. "No place like home," he said. He sat there, very pleased with himself, surrounded by the girls.

"If you're not afraid to go home in the dark," said Laura Sharp.

"By myself, I am," he said.

They sat until they heard the last tram. In a few minutes, Emma Houselay came in.

"Come to the fire, Emma," said Polly Birkin.

"It's really cold outside," said Emma.

"Who are you going with tonight, John Thomas?" said Muriel.

"Tonight? Oh, I'm going home by myself tonight," he said.

They laughed. He got up and reached for his coat.

"I'm going," he said.

"No, don't go," said Polly. "We're all here waiting for you."

"We've all got to get up early in the morning," he said.

"But don't leave us, John Thomas," said Muriel. "Take one of us!"

"I'll take you all if you like," he said.

"Oh no," said Muriel. "Two's company. Seven's too many."

"Take one of us," said Laura. "Say which."

"Yes," said Annie, speaking for the first time. "Choose, John Thomas. Let's hear you."

23

"No," he said. "I'm going home by myself tonight. I'm going to be good, tonight."

"You've got to take one of us," said Annie.

"No, no," he said, laughing uneasily. "I don't want to make enemies."

"You'll only make one enemy," said Annie.

"She means the one you choose," added Laura.

John Thomas turned, as if to escape. "Well, goodnight," he said.

"No," said Muriel. "You must choose. Turn your face to the wall, and one of us will touch you. You must say which. Go on, turn your face to the wall, and don't look."

He didn't like it. He didn't trust them. But he was not brave enough to go. They pushed him to a wall and made him stand there. They stood behind him, and laughed at him.

Then suddenly Annie, with a movement like a cat, went forward and hit him hard on the side of the head. His cap fell off and he turned round.

Then they all attacked him; they hit him, and pulled his hair. But it was like a game. They were not angry.

But he was angry. His blue eyes burned with anger, and with fear, too. He pushed past them to the door, but it was locked. So he faced them like a hunted animal.

"Come on," shouted Annie. "Choose, choose."

"What do you want? Open the door," he said.

"Not until you've chosen," said Muriel.

"Chosen what?"

"The girl you're going to marry," she replied.

"No, open the door, and behave yourselves," he said.

"You've got to choose," they shouted.

"Come on," said Annie. "Come on." She looked straight at him.

He went forward uncertainly. Annie had taken off her belt and she hit him on the head with it. He jumped at her and held her. But immediately the other girls rushed at him, pulling and tearing and hitting him over and over again. Now they were really angry. Now they wanted their revenge. His coat and shirt were torn. Nora held the back of his neck. At last, he was down on the floor. They jumped on him. He could not breathe or move, and his face was bleeding.

The girls' faces were red, their hair was wild, their eyes shone strangely, they were breathless. At last John Thomas lay quite still, like an animal that cannot escape.

"Now!" said Annie.

There was a dead silence.

"Now you know," said Annie. "Now you know what you've done, don't you. You know what you've done."

He lay with his face turned away and did not answer.

"You ought to be killed," she said in a low voice. "You ought to be killed."

Some of the girls were laughing. Then Polly said, "He's got to choose."

"Did you hear?" said Annie. "Did you hear?"

She shook him and hit him hard across the face. He did not answer.

"Did you hear?" she repeated.

"What?" he said. He was afraid.

"Choose your girl, choose her now, or I'll break your neck. There'll be no more of your tricks."

But although he was down, and although he

was afraid, he didn't give in. No, he would not give in. They could tear him in pieces.

"All right," he said. He smiled, an unkind smile. "I choose Annie."

Annie stepped back at once.

"He's chosen Annie!" shouted the girls.

"Me?" said Annie. "Me?" she repeated in a strange hard voice. "I wouldn't touch him."

But she felt a deep pain. She nearly fell. He lay there in his torn clothes, with his bleeding face, his head turned away.

"Oh, if he's chosen," said Polly. "Let him go."

"I don't want him. He can choose again," said Annie.

"Get up," said Polly. "Get up."

He rose slowly, a strange, shocked man. The girls watched him.

"Who wants him?" said Laura roughly.

"Nobody," they said. But each of them was waiting and hoping, hoping he would look at her. All except Annie. Something was broken in her.

It was the end. Slowly he found his cap and his heavy coat, and stood by the locked door in silence.

"Open the door, somebody," said Laura.

"Annie's got the key," said Nora. She took the key from Annie and unlocked the door.

"Don't be angry," she said.

Without a word, he opened the door, and went.

"That'll teach him," said Laura.

"Yes, it will," said Nora.

"Shut up!" cried Annie, as if in pain.

"Well," said Muriel. "I'm ready to go, Polly. Come on, hurry up."

They all wanted to go. They put on their coats

26

and hats hurriedly, and went out, in a shocked, unbelieving silence.

The Rocking-Horse Winner

There was a woman who was beautiful and who came from a comfortable home. Yet she had no luck. She married for love, and the love died. She had pretty, healthy children, but she did not want them and could not love them. Everyone said, "She's such a good mother." Only she and her children knew that in the centre of her heart was a cold, hard little place, that could not love.

She had a boy and two little girls. They lived in a pleasant house, with a garden, and they had servants who cooked the meals and cleaned the house.

But there was always a worry in the house. There was never enough money. The father worked in an office, and the mother had a little money too; but they had to live as if they were rich. So there was always a shortage of money.

The mother worried and worried because her children were growing up, and they must go to expensive schools. The mother and father both liked expensive clothes and food and furniture and holidays. But the father could not earn more, and neither could the mother. So there was always a whisper in the air. There must be more money! There must be more money! No-one said it, but they all heard it.

The children could hear it all the time. They heard it at Christmas, when there were expensive toys. The whisper seemed to come from the shining new rocking-horse, and the big toy train, and the smart new dolls. The secret whisper was all over the house. There must be more money.

"Mother," said the boy Paul one day. "Why do we always use Uncle Oscar's car, or take a taxi? Why haven't we got our own car?"

"Because we're poor," said his mother.

"But why are we poor, Mother?"

"Well, I suppose," she said slowly, "it's because your father has no luck."

The boy was silent for some time. Then he asked,

"Is luck the same as money?"

"No, Paul. Not quite. Luck is what makes you have money."

"Oh."

"If you're lucky, you will always have money."

"And Father is unlucky? Why?"

"I don't know. No-one knows why one person is lucky and another isn't."

"Not God?"

"Perhaps God. But He never tells."

"He ought to. Aren't you lucky either, Mother?"

"I can't be lucky, if I married an unlucky husband. I used to think I was, before I married. Now I think I'm very unlucky indeed."

The child looked at her, at her unhappy face and the lines round her mouth.

"Well I'm lucky," he said. "I'm a lucky person."

"Why?" said his mother, with a sudden laugh.

He stared at her. He didn't know why he had said it.

"God told me," he said.

"I hope he did, dear," she said.

"He did!"

"Then that's excellent!" she said.

The boy knew she did not believe him. He was not important. He felt angry. He wanted her to notice him. He went away by himself. He looked for luck. He wanted it, he wanted it, he wanted it. The two little girls were playing with their dolls. He sat on his rocking-horse, rocking wildly. His eyes had a strange look, and the little girls didn't dare speak to him.

When he had ridden to the end of his mad little journey, he said to the rocking-horse, "Now, take me to somewhere lucky! Take me!" He knew, he knew the horse could take him to a lucky place. So he got on his horse again and began another angry ride.

"You'll break your horse, Paul," said the children's nurse.

"He's always riding like that. I wish he'd stop," said his sister Joan.

But he only stared at them in silence.

One day his Uncle Oscar came in, when Paul was riding.

"Are you riding a winner?" he said.

Paul said nothing. At last he stopped the horse and got off it.

"I got there," he said.

"Where?"

"Where I wanted to go."

"What's the horse's name?" said Uncle Oscar.

"He doesn't have a name. I mean, he has different names. Last week he was called Sansovino."

"Sansovino?" said his uncle. "That's the name of the horse that won the big race at Ascot."

"He's always talking about horse-races to Bassett," said Joan.

Bassett was the young gardener. Uncle Oscar went to see him. He had once been Uncle Oscar's servant. He knew a lot about horse-racing.

"Master Paul comes and asks me about the names of the race-horses," he said. He was very serious, as if he was talking about God.

"Does he ever bet on a horse? Does he ever win any money?"

"You must ask him, sir," said Bassett.

So Uncle Oscar took Paul for a ride in his car.

"Paul," he asked, "do you ever bet on race-horses?"

"Why?" said Paul. "Is it wrong?"

"No, not at all. Can you tell me who's going to win the big race at Lincoln?"

"Daffodil," said Paul.

"Daffodil? I don't think so. What about Mirza?"

"I only know the winner," said Paul. "That's Daffodil." There was a pause. Daffodil was not a well-known horse.

"Uncle?"

"Yes?"

30

"Don't tell anyone. I promised Bassett."

"Bassett?"

"We bet together. You gave me ten shillings at Christmas, remember? Bassett put it on a horse for me and I won."

"I see. How much are you going to bet on Daffodil?"

"All my money except twenty pounds."

"How much are you betting, then?"

"Three hundred pounds."

"*What*? Where's the money?"

"Bassett keeps it for me."

Between wonder and amusement Uncle Oscar was silent. Then he said, "I'll take you to the Lincoln race-meeting."

So they went to the races together. Paul had never been to a race-meeting before, and his eyes were like blue fire.

"Now," said Uncle Oscar, "I'm going to put twenty pounds on Mirza. I'll put five pounds for you, on any horse you choose."

"Daffodil."

"Are you sure?"

"Yes."

Daffodil was first and Mirza was third. Uncle Oscar brought Paul four five-pound notes. "Now what?" he said.

"I must talk to Bassett," said Paul. "I have fifteen hundred pounds now, and twenty, and this twenty. You see, Bassett's lucky. And you must be lucky too, Uncle, because I started winning when you gave me that ten shillings. You could bet with us, if you like, Uncle."

Uncle Oscar took Paul and Bassett into the park for the afternoon, and there they talked.

"We've been putting money on horses for about a year now, sir. We lost at first. Then you gave Master Paul that ten shillings. We put it on Singhalese, and the horse won. And since then, we've nearly always won, haven't we, Master Paul?"

"If we're sure, then it's all right, then we win," said Paul.

"But when are you sure?" said Uncle Oscar, smiling.

"It's Master Paul, sir," said Bassett. "It's as if God told him."

"And you keep the money?"

"It's quite safe, sir. Master Paul can have it when he wants it."

"Fifteen hundred pounds?"

"And forty more," said Paul.

"If Master Paul wants you to join us, then you should, sir," said Bassett.

Oscar thought about it. They went home, and Bassett showed him the money.

"It's all right when we're sure, Uncle," said Paul again. Uncle Oscar was puzzled. But he joined them. Before the St. Leger race-meeting, Paul was 'sure' about a horse called Lively Spark. It was not the favourite, and no-one thought it would win. Paul bet a thousand pounds, Bassett five hundred, and Uncle Oscar two hundred.

Lively Spark won, and Paul had made ten thousand pounds.

"You see?" he said. "I was quite sure of him."

Uncle Oscar had made two thousand pounds.

"What are you going to do with your money?" he said.

"It's for mother. She said that she and father are unlucky. I thought, if I were lucky, the whispering would stop."

"Whispering?"

"The house," said Paul. "I hate our house."

"What does it whisper?"

"I don't know, but the house is always short of money."

"I know, Paul, I know."

"Mother gets a lot of bills. She can't pay them and then she gets letters from lawyers."

"I know," said Uncle Oscar.

"And then the house whispers. It's like people laughing at you, behind your back. It's horrible."

"Does your mother know that you talk to Bassett about racing?" said Uncle Oscar.

"Yes, I think so, but she doesn't know about the money. I don't want her to know."

"Why not?"

"She might stop me."

"I don't think she would."

"Don't tell her, Uncle, don't."

"All right," said Uncle Oscar. "All right."

Paul had a plan, and Uncle Oscar helped him. Paul gave his uncle five thousand pounds, and Uncle Oscar gave it to the family lawyer.

The family lawyer wrote to Paul's mother. The letter said that a relation wanted to give her a thousand pounds, on her birthday, every year for five years.

Paul's mother's birthday was in November. The house had been whispering a lot recently, so Paul waited anxiously for the birthday letter.

At breakfast on the morning of her birthday, Paul watched his mother's face. When she read the lawyer's letter, her face became hard and cold. She said nothing.

"Did you have any nice letters for your birthday, Mother?" said Paul.

"Quite nice," said his mother. She said no more, but that morning she went to London.

She went to see the lawyer.

In the afternoon Uncle Oscar appeared.

"She wants all the money now, at once," he told Paul.

"Shall I give it to her, Uncle?"

"It's your decision, Paul."

"Let her have it, then," said Paul. "We can get some more. There's the Grand National, and the Lincoln, and the Derby. I'm sure I'll know one of the winners."

So Uncle Oscar went to see the lawyer, and Paul's mother had the five thousand pounds.

Then something very strange happened.

The whispering voices in the house grew louder and louder. There was new furniture. Paul had private lessons from a teacher, because he was going to go to a big expensive school. It was winter, but the house was full of spring flowers. And still the whispers grew louder and louder. There must be more money, oh now, now, there must be more money, more than ever!

Paul was frightened. He worked hard with his teacher, but he spent a lot of time with Bassett. Summer came. The Grand National and the Lincoln races were over, and Paul had not been

34

'sure'. They had lost money.

Paul's eyes became wild and strange. "I've got to know for the Derby, I've got to know!" he said.

His mother noticed that he was not well

"Would you like to go to the seaside, for a holiday?" she said.

"Oh no, Mother, I can't go before the Derby, not before the Derby."

"Why not? Paul, I think you care too much about these races. People in my family used to lose a lot of money, betting on horses. It's caused a lot of trouble. I shall send Bassett away, and I shall ask Uncle Oscar not to take you to any more race-meetings. You must promise to go to the seaside, and forget the races."

"I can't leave the house, Mother, not before the Derby," Paul repeated.

"Can't leave the house? I didn't know you loved it." Paul looked at her without speaking. He had a secret within a secret. He had not told either Uncle Oscar or Bassett about it.

"All right," said his mother at last. "But you must promise to forget about horses and racing. Promise."

"Don't worry, Mother," said Paul. "Don't worry. You needn't worry, really."

Paul's great secret was his wooden rocking-horse, the horse with no name. It was in his bedroom at the top of the house.

"You're too old to play with a rocking-horse," his mother said. "I like him," said Paul. "Let me keep him until I can have a real horse."

The Derby came nearer and nearer. Paul became more and more strange. He was thin, and his eyes seemed very big. Sometimes his mother was really uneasy about him. Sometimes, for half an hour, she would suddenly feel very anxious. Then she wanted to go to him, and save him from something. But from what?

Two nights before the Derby, she was at a big party in London. Suddenly, she felt very worried about Paul. She left the dance, and telephoned the house. But the children's nurse said that Paul was well, and in bed.

It was about one o'clock when Paul's mother and father came home. She went upstairs to her son's room. She listened at the door. There was a noise, heavy, strange, not loud. What was it? Something huge, something powerful was moving. Cold with anxiety and fear, she opened the door. The room was dark, yet something was moving backwards and forwards. She switched on the light.

Paul was madly riding the rocking-horse.

"Paul, what are you doing?" she cried.

"It's Malabar," he screamed, in a voice she didn't know. "It's Malabar!"

Then he fell with a crash to the ground. She rushed to pick him up and hold him. His eyes were closed and his face was white; he seemed very ill, and she put him to bed.

"What did he mean, Malabar?" she asked his father.

"I don't know."

She asked Uncle Oscar.

"Malabar is one of the horses running in the Derby," said Uncle Oscar. And he went to Bassett, and bet a thousand pounds on Malabar.

On Derby Day, Paul was still very ill. He did not sleep or speak, and his eyes were like blue stones. His mother sat near him, feeling that her heart had become a stone.

In the evening, Bassett came to the house. He wanted to see Paul. His mother was angry, but she let him come in. Perhaps he could help Paul.

The gardener came and stood by Paul's bed, staring at the restless, dying child.

"Master Paul," he whispered. "Master Paul. Malabar was first, Malabar won. You've made more than seventy thousand pounds. Malabar won, Master Paul."

"Malabar, Malabar," cried the child. "Did I say Malabar? Do you think I'm lucky, Mother? Over seventy thousand pounds, that's lucky, isn't it Mother? I was sure, I *knew*. If I ride my rocking-horse till I'm sure, it's all right, isn't it Bassett? Did you put something on Malabar, Bassett?"

"Yes, Master Paul. I put a thousand pounds on it."

"I never told you about my horse, Mother," said Paul. "If I ride my horse long enough, then I'm sure, quite sure. Mother, am I lucky? Am I really lucky? Didn't I tell you?"

"No, you didn't tell me," said his mother.

Paul died in the night. While he lay there, Uncle Oscar said to the mother, "You've got seventy thousand pounds, and lost your son. But poor child, poor child, it's best he's gone, it's best. He's best out of this world, out of a life where he has to ride a rocking-horse to find a winner."

You Touched Me

Matilda and Emmie Rockley were unmarried.
They lived in a square ugly brick house, which
belonged to a big pottery. But the factory was
empty; no-one made pots there now.

"We like it better – much better – it's quieter,"
said Matilda.

"Oh yes," agreed Emmie.

The house was quieter, it was true; but did
Matilda and Emmie really like it? Perhaps they
missed the noise of the pottery workers, the shouting girls. Certainly their lives were grey and com-
fortless now.

In a factory town it is not easy to find the right
husbands. There were plenty of young men, but
they were all factory workers. The Rockley girls
would have about £10,000 each, after their
father's death. It was a lot of money. They would
have married a minister, or a teacher, or a bank-
clerk. But no professional man asked them.
Matilda thought she would always live in the
Pottery House.

Matilda was tall, thin, and fair, with a rather
long nose. She loved painting and music, and read

39

a lot of books. Emmie looked after the house. She could not play the piano or paint, and she admired Matilda.

Their mother was dead, and their father was getting old. The three of them, with one servant-girl, lived together, year after year. Friends came, their father drank whisky and became ill. He was slowly dying. He was an intelligent man, and had some education, but he preferred to think that he was just one of the factory workers.

In their quiet, sad way, the girls were not unhappy. But there was one problem. Ted Rockley had no son, and he wanted one. When the girls were growing up, he went to London. He came back with a boy of six, Hadrian.

Hadrian had no father or mother, and he came from a home for orphans like himself. He was an ordinary boy, with ordinary blue-ish eyes and brownish hair. Matilda and Emmie didn't like him, and he knew this. But they were not unkind, and Hadrian grew up in the Pottery House, went to school in the town, and was always called Hadrian Rockley.

Matilda wanted him to be a gentleman. But he would not. He ran away from school, sold his books and his school clothes, and spent the money.

When he was fifteen, he said he wanted to leave England. So he went to Canada. He said goodbye to the Rockleys without a word of thanks, and left them, it seemed, without a tear. But he wrote fairly regularly from Canada. He had a job in a factory, something to do with electricity, and he did well.

At last, however, the war came. Hadrian joined

the army and came to Europe. He did not visit the Pottery House. But Ted Rockley was dying, and he wanted to see Hadrian. In 1918, when the war was over, Hadrian wrote a letter. He said he was coming home to the Pottery House.

The girls were anxious; they were a little afraid of Hadrian. They had been nursing their father, and they were both tired. Hadrian was a young man of twenty-one, who had left them coldly five years before. They did not want him.

They began to make the house ready. Emmie moved her father's bed downstairs, and his room upstairs was prepared for Hadrian. Both girls were busy cleaning the house when, at ten o'clock in the morning, Hadrian suddenly arrived.

He walked in with his suitcase. He was little, neat, sure of himself, and not at all shy.

Matilda was in the kitchen, and wearing her working clothes, with a duster round her head. When she saw Hadrian, her face reddened, but she dried her hands and went forward.

"Hadrian," she said. "We thought you were coming tomorrow. How are you?"

"Quite well thank you."

"You're a man now," she said.

Hadrian looked at her. She didn't look pretty; thin, with her large nose, and the duster round her head. She knew this, but she didn't mind. She had seen a lot of suffering, and she didn't mind unhappiness any more. She was used to it.

"Come and see my father," she said.

In the hall they met Emmie. She was on the stairs, brushing them. Her hand went up to her hair.

"Why have you come today?" she said. "We're

41

in the middle of the housework."

"I came away a day earlier," said Hadrian. His man's voice was deep. It surprised Emmie. It was like a blow to her.

They went into Mr Rockley's room. He was dressed, but he was resting on the bed, near the window. From there, he could see his beautiful garden. He didn't look as ill as he was, but still he looked old, a wreck. He smiled at Hadrian.

"Well," he said. "You're not tall enough for a soldier. Do you want something to eat?"

"I don't mind," said Hadrian.

"What will you have? Egg and bacon?" asked Emmie shortly.

"Yes, I don't mind," said Hadrian.

The sisters went to the kitchen, and sent the servant to finish the stairs.

"Isn't he different," said Matilda.

"Isn't he!" said Emmie. "What a little man."

They both laughed uneasily.

"Oh, he's not bad," said Matilda.

"He's all right," said Emmie. "But he's very pleased with himself."

"He caught us in the middle of the housework."

"Oh, men don't think," said Emmie. "Go and get dressed, Matilda, I don't care about him. I'll do the cooking, and you can talk to him."

"He'll talk to my father," said Matilda.

"Yes," said Emmie, making a face. "He will."

The sisters believed that Hadrian wanted something from their father. They thought he was hoping for some money when Mr Rockley died. And they thought he might get it.

Matilda went upstairs to change. She dressed

very carefully, arranging her long fair hair, putting on a soft green dress and a string of pearls, and a little make-up. Now she looked like a woman in a magazine story, as beautiful and almost as unreal.

She found Hadrian and her father talking like old friends. Hadrian was telling him about Canada.

"I'm going back when my holiday is over," he said.

"You don't want to stop in England?" said Mr Rockley.

"No."

"Why not? There are plenty of jobs."

"Yes, but there's too much difference between the workers and the owners."

The sick man looked at him with smiling eyes.

"That's the reason, is it?"

Matilda heard and understood. She went down to the kitchen.

"He's so pleased with himself, he thinks he's wonderful," she said to Emmie. "He doesn't want to stay here. He thinks there's too much difference between masters and men here."

"Is it different in Canada?"

"Oh yes. He thinks everyone's on the same level in Canada."

"Well," said Emmie. "He's here now. So he can keep his proper place. He won't be master here."

As they talked, they saw the young man walking slowly down the garden, looking at the flowers. He had his hands in his pockets and his soldier's cap neatly on his head.

"We know why he's here," said Emmie.

Matilda looked for a long time at the neat young

43

man.

"You don't know, Emmie. Perhaps he's not come for money."

Matilda's dark blue eyes had a strange look in them. She held her head high, but she had a look of pain.

That afternoon their father seemed weak and ill. The doctor came, and told Matilda that her father might die suddenly. They must be prepared.

The day passed, and the next. Hadrian behaved like a son of the house.

On the second day after Hadrian's arrival, Matilda sat with her father in the evening. She was drawing, copying a picture. It was very quiet. Hadrian had gone out, no-one knew where, and Emmie was busy. Mr Rockley looked out in silence at his garden in the evening sun.

"If anything happens to me, Matilda," he said, "you won't sell this house. You'll stay here . . . "

Matilda stared at him.

"We couldn't do anything else," she said.

"You don't know what you might do. I've left everything to you and Emmie. You can do what you like with the money. But don't sell this house."

"No."

"And give Hadrian my watch, and a hundred pounds, and help him if he wants help."

"Your watch, and a hundred pounds, and help him if he wants help. But you'll still be here when he goes back to Canada, Father."

"You don't know," said her father.

Matilda sat and watched him for a long time. She understood that he might die soon.

become an old woman, she was finished. And Cecilia thought, "Now she can live as she really is. This is what she really is."

Pauline stayed in her room. She told the servant to take away all the mirrors.

Robert and Cecilia sat together a lot, but Cecilia did not dare tell him what she had done.

"Do you think your mother ever loved anybody?" she said to him one evening.

"She loved herself," he said at last.

"But she didn't," cried Cecilia. "She didn't like herself. What did she love?"

"Power," he said shortly.

"What power? I don't understand."

"She fed on other lives. She was beautiful. Life was her food. Henry's life. My life."

"And you don't forgive her?"

"No."

"Poor Aunt Pauline."

"I know I have a heart," he said. "But it's almost empty."

Cecilia was silent. What could she say?

Two days later, Pauline took too much sleeping medicine, and died.

But even from her grave she hit back at her son and her niece. She left Robert one thousand pounds. She left Cecilia one hundred.

All the rest and all her treasures went to make 'The Pauline Attenborough Museum'.

Tickets Please

There was once, in the Midlands of England, a single-line tramway. It went from the city into the country, past black factories, up and down hills, through villages of workmen's houses, past churches, over rivers and railways, downhill to where the coal-mines are. Then it went uphill again, and rushed on to its stopping-place. This was a cold, ugly little town, full of factories, on the edge of wild dark country.

There in the little town, the tram-cars, painted green and cream, paused. They seemed pleased with themselves.

But after a few minutes they started again on their adventure, on and on for two long hours, all the way back to the coal-mines and to the city again.

It was always an adventure. Because it was 1915 and war-time, the drivers were men that the army did not want. So they drove very fast, careless of danger. People said it was the most dangerous tram-line in England.

The tickets were taken by girls, and they, in their ugly dark-blue clothing, were never afraid. The tram might be packed with shouting miners, upstairs and down; but the girls didn't mind.

They shouted back at young men who didn't pay for their tickets. They feared no-one, and everybody was afraid of them.

Annie was one of these girls. She liked the adventure. The best time was between ten o'clock in the morning and one in the afternoon. Not many people took the trams then, and Annie could look around her. Sometimes she jumped off the car and ran into a shop, and the driver waited for her. The girls and the drivers were good friends, companions in danger, like sailors on a ship in stormy seas.

The inspector, the man who checked the money, was young too. There were no grey heads. Tall, with a small dark-brown moustache, he used to jump on the tram and greet Annie, and they had a good, easy, eighteen-kilometre talk.

The inspector's name was John Thomas. There was a lot of talk in the villages about John Thomas. He talked and laughed with the girls in the mornings, and walked in the fields with them in the dark night, when they left the trams. Most of the girls were pretty, and they were like sailors. What did it matter, what they did in port? They would soon be at sea again.

However, Annie was not an easy girl. She had a sharp tongue, and for several months, she had refused to walk with John Thomas. Perhaps this was because she liked him. He did not stop asking her, with a little smile on his face.

One November night, Annie was free. There was a fair in the city every November. It was a wet, ugly night, but she put on her best clothes and went to the fairground. She was alone, but she hoped to find a friend.

John Thomas was the first man to greet her. He was smiling, as usual. She was glad to see him. He took her on one of the roundabouts. It was not as exciting as riding in a tram-car, but, sitting there with John Thomas, Annie was quite happy.

He paid for a second ride. So when he put his arm round her, she could not push him away.

They went on another roundabout, and then they went all round the fair, and then they went to the cinema.

Of course, it is very dark in a cinema. John Thomas and Annie sat close together. She wanted

Later, she told Emmie.

"Why should Hadrian have Father's watch?" said Emmie. "Let him take the money and go." She loved her father.

That night Matilda sat late in her room. Her heart was anxious and sad. She could not cry, but all the time she thought of her father, only her father. At last she felt she must go to him.

It was near midnight. She went along the passage to his room. There was a faint light from the moon. She listened at his door. Then she softly opened it and entered. The room was not quite dark.

"Are you asleep?" she whispered, going to the side of the bed.

"Are you asleep?" She put out her hand and touched his head gently. "Can't you sleep tonight?"

There was a movement in the bed.

"Yes, I can," a voice answered. It was Hadrian's voice.

Instantly she remembered. Her father was sleeping downstairs and Hadrian had his room. She stood still.

"Is it you, Hadrian? I thought it was my father."

The young man gave an uncomfortable laugh, and turned in the bed.

At last she got out of the room. When she was back in her own room, and the door was closed, she stood holding up her hand, as if it were hurt.

"Well," said her mind. "It was only a mistake. Don't take any notice of it."

But she was in pain. Her hand hurt. She could not forgive Hadrian; she disliked him deeply.

45

Hadrian too could not sleep. The soft hand moving through his hair had given him a strange feeling in his heart. He was an orphan, he had no real home, he was against the world. The gentle touch showed him unknown things.

In the morning Matilda saw him looking at her. She tried to behave as if she didn't care. She looked at him without warmth, and with her long fine hand, she put sugar in his coffee.

But she could not control him. He remembered; he had new feelings. Something new was awake and watchful in him. He had a secret.

He looked at her. She was not beautiful, but her skin was clear and fine, her hands narrow and white. She was somehow above him, and he wanted to be her master. She was like her father; she had his quality. He went about the house and garden, planning secretly.

Matilda knew he watched her. She felt him following her like a shadow. But she would not notice him. She behaved as if he was a young boy, who lived in their house, but was a stranger. She dared not remember his head under her hand. She wanted to forget it. She thought she had forgotten it.

One day, when he sat with Mr Rockley, he looked straight into the eyes of the sick man and said,

"I wouldn't like to live and die here, in this town."

"You needn't."

"Does Matilda like it?"

"I think so," said the sick man.

"It's not a very interesting life for her. How

46

much older is she than me?"

"Quite a lot."

"Over thirty?"

"She's thirty-two."

Hadrian thought for a minute.

"She doesn't seem older," he said.

The sick man looked at him.

"Do you think she'd like to leave here?" said Hadrian.

"I don't know," said Mr Rockley restlessly.

Hadrian sat still. Then in a small quiet voice, which came from inside him, he said,

"I would marry her, if you wanted it."

The sick man stared at him for a long time.

"You?" he said.

"If you are not against it."

"No, I'm not against it. I've never thought of it. But Emmie's the youngest."

He smiled; he was pleased. Secretly, he loved the boy.

They were both silent. Then Emmie came in and they talked about other things.

For two days Mr Rockley was excited and thoughtful. Hadrian was very quiet.

At last the father and Matilda were alone together. It was very early in the morning, and Mr Rockley had had a lot of pain.

"Matilda," he said suddenly.

"I'm here."

"I want you to do something. I want you to marry Hadrian."

She was frightened. She thought he wasn't in his right mind.

"Sit still, sit still," he said. "Listen."

"But you don't know what you're saying,

Father."

"I do. I want you to marry Hadrian."

She looked at him slowly.

"Why?" she said. "Where did this idea come from?"

"From him."

"It's a shocking idea."

"The boy's all right."

"Tell him to go away," she said coldly.

He did not answer, but looked out of the window. At last he turned back to her. He looked really angry with her.

"If you won't marry him, you're a fool. And I'll make you pay for your foolishness."

She was cold with fear. She could not believe him.

"I mean it," he said. "If you won't marry him, you'll have nothing when I die. Not you, and not Emmie."

She left him, and went to her room, and locked the door.

She stayed there for several hours. At last, in the evening, she told Emmie.

"That devil Hadrian," said Emmie. "He wants the money." Matilda did not love Hadrian, but she had never thought that he was devilish. Now she was afraid of him.

Emmie talked to her father next day.

"Do you mean it, Father?" she said.

"Yes."

"You don't."

He looked at her with a little smile.

"I do. Nothing for you and nothing for Matilda."

Hadrian was in the garden. Emmie went to him.

"Go away," she said. "Take your things and go. Quick."

"Who says I must go?"

"We do."

"Your father too?"

"Yes, he does."

"I'll ask him."

"No, you needn't ask him. We don't want you here. So you can go."

"He's the master here."

"He's dying," she said. "And you stay here, trying to get his money."

"Who says that?"

"I do. And Matilda knows, too. So get out of this house."

He turned his back to her, and began to think. He did want the money, very badly. He wanted to be an owner and not a worker. But he didn't want Matilda because of the money. He wanted both. He didn't want Matilda without the money. But he didn't want her because of the money.

When he thought he understood this, he waited. He wanted to tell her.

In the evening, the lawyer came. Mr Rockley made a new will. Unless Matilda agreed to marry Hadrian, then, after six months, Hadrian would have everything, the house and the money.

He told Hadrian this. "Tell Matilda," said Hadrian.

The two daughters came, white-faced and silent. Their father showed them the will. "There it is," he said.

49

The two women sat without speaking. They did not look at the paper.

"Either Matilda marries Hadrian, or he has everything," said their father.

"He can have everything," said Matilda coldly.

"No, no," said Emmie, ready to fight.

"I didn't want to marry Matilda because of the money," said Hadrian.

"You did," cried Emmie.

"She knows I didn't," said Hadrian.

Emmie looked at her sister.

"Don't worry, Matilda," she said. "Let him have everything."

"He'll take everything," said Matilda.

It was true. Hadrian knew he would take everything.

"Isn't he clever," said Emmie. "What a clever little man. What a clever little devil."

The father smiled, but he was tired.

"Go away," he said. "Let me be quiet."

Another night passed. A nurse came. Mr Rockley was in bad pain, and the end was near.

The girls and Hadrian were very quiet. None of them would give in. Hadrian thought, and was satisfied. If he didn't marry Matilda, he would have twenty thousand pounds. If he did marry her, she would have her own money.

He wanted to speak to Matilda alone, and at last he found her in the garden. She was picking fruit. He stood in front of her and she could not escape.

"Don't you want me, Matilda?" he said.

"I don't want to speak to you."

"You put your hand on me," he said. "If you hadn't done that, I wouldn't have thought of you. But you touched me."

"That was a mistake. If you were a good man, you would know that, and forget it."

"I do know it, but I can't forget it. You woke me up. I can't go to sleep again."

"You should have gone away."

"I didn't want to."

She looked away. "I'm old enough to be your mother," she said.

"It doesn't matter. You're not my mother. Marry me, and let's go to Canada. Why not? You touched me."

But she walked away from him. He felt angry and sad.

That evening she went to her father's room.

"Yes," she said suddenly. "I'll marry him."

Her father was in pain, and very ill.

"You like him now, do you?" he said with a faint smile.

She looked down at her father's face. She saw that death was not far off.

The lawyer was sent for. Arrangements were made. Emmie shouted and cried, but Matilda was silent and unmoved. Hadrian was quietly pleased with himself, and a little afraid.

After two more days, they were married. After the wedding Matilda and Hadrian came straight home and went into the room of the dying man.

He smiled at them, there was a light in his eyes.

"Hadrian, you've got her," he said.

"Yes," said Hadrian. His face was very white.

51

"I'm glad you're my son," whispered the dying man. He turned to Matilda. "Let me look at you, Matilda," he said. Then his voice changed. "Kiss me," he said.

She bent and kissed him.

"Kiss him," said her father.

She kissed her young husband.

"That's right, that's right," whispered the dying man.

The White Stocking

"I'm getting up, Teddy," said Mrs Whiston, and she jumped out of bed.

"What's the matter with you?" asked Whiston.

"Nothing," she said brightly. "Can't I get up?"

It was about seven o'clock, and hardly light yet, in the cold bedroom. Whiston lay still and looked at his wife. She was a pretty little thing, with her short black hair. She dressed quickly, throwing on her clothes. She stood in front of the mirror and roughly combed her hair. He watched the quick movement of her soft young shoulders, quietly, like a husband.

"Get up," she said, turning to him. "Get up. Rise and shine!"

They had been married two years. But still, when she went out of the room, he felt as if all his

52

light and warmth went too. He began to notice the cold damp morning. He got up, wondering why she was so early. Usually she lay in bed as late as she could.

Whiston went downstairs in his shirt and trousers. He went down the narrow hall into the kitchen of their small cheap house, their first home. He was a tall young man of about twenty-eight, sleepy now, and feeling good. She was singing. She filled the kettle and washed last night's cups for breakfast. She looked like a careless young woman, but she was quite a good housewife.

"Ted," she said.

"What?"

"Light a fire, quick."

He began to put paper and sticks into the fireplace.

Suddenly there was a loud knock at the door.

"I'll go," said Elsie.

It was the postman. He smiled at her and gave her some small parcels. "St. Valentine's Day, February 14th," he said. "Your secret lovers haven't forgotten you."

"No," she said, and closed the door in his face.

She was only interested in her post.

She tore open a long thin envelope. There was a very ugly greeting-card inside. She smiled and dropped it on the floor. Then she opened a little parcel. Inside was a white box, and inside that a white silk handkerchief with the letter E on it. Elsie smiled pleasantly and put the box down. The third envelope contained another white packet. Inside there seemed to be another handkerchief. She shook it. It was a long white stocking. There was a little weight in the toe. She put her arm into the stocking and brought out a box. She looked inside, then quickly opened a door and went into the little cold sitting-room. With a pleased smile she lifted a pair of pearl earrings from the box, and went to the mirror. She put the earrings in her ears, looking at herself sideways in the glass. She shook her head and watched the earrings dance. They were cold against her neck. She smiled at herself in the mirror, and then laughed.

There was a piece of paper in the box. On it was written:

'Pearls are fair, but you are fairer.
Wear these for me, and I'll love the wearer.'

She made a funny face, and went to the mirror again. Whiston came in. He didn't see much, he was still sleepy. His voice was warm and slow. His eyes were very blue, very kind.

"What've you got?" he said.

"Valentines," she said. "It's Valentine's day so I get presents from my boyfriends." She showed him the handkerchief.

"Who gave you this?" he said.

"It's a valentine," she said. "People don't put their names on valentines. I don't know who sent it."

"You know," he said.

"I don't! I don't!"

He was displeased. "You're married now," he said. "They shouldn't send you valentines."

"Ted! Why not?"

"You know who sent it," he said again.

"I don't, truly!"

54

He looked round, and saw the white stocking on a chair.

"Is this another valentine?"

"No, no," she said. "That's just something from a shop."

She fetched the greeting card. "Look, there's a card, too."

He looked at it. "They're fools," he said.

He went out of the room, and she flew upstairs and took off the earrings.

In the kitchen, he was on his knees in front of the fire.

"This fire's slow."

She put her arms round his neck.

"And who else is slow?"

"One of us, I know," he said. He got up carefully. Her arms were still round his neck and she was lifted off her feet.

"Swing me!" she said.

She hung round his neck, laughing. Then she dropped off. "The water's boiling," she sang, and ran for the teapot. He smiled at her.

At breakfast, she stopped smiling.

"Teddy."

"What?"

"I told you a lie."

"Oh yes?"

"Yes."

He cut a piece of bread.

"Was it a good lie?"

She laughed. Then she thought.

"No, not very good."

"Tell me then," he said. His voice was warm.

"That white stocking," she said. "That was a valentine too."

He looked serious.

"Then why did you lie?" There was a little anger in his voice.

"I was afraid."

"You weren't."

"I was, Teddy."

There was a pause.

"Who sent it?" he asked.

"I can guess," she said. "But there wasn't a name."

She ran to the sitting-room and came back with the piece of paper.

He read it twice. His face became a dull red.

"Who sent it?"

"I think Sam Adams," she said.

He was silent for a moment.

"Fool," he said. "And what's he talking about, pearls? And why 'wear these for me'? There's only one stocking."

"He sent me one last year," she said. "So now I have a pair."

"Did he send you a white stocking last year?"

"Yes. I thought you would be angry, if I told you." He got up and began washing himself at the kitchen tap.

She moved quickly, taking the breakfast things off the table, and she watched him. She loved him, she loved his face. He was so sure, so safe. She knew she was in his power. She could do anything, since he loved her.

He turned round.

"Have you been meeting him? Have you?"

"Yes," she said, after a moment. "Once. He got into the tram with me, one morning, and we had coffee at the Royal Hotel."

"Did you?"

"Yes. It was cold. It was nice at the Royal."

"You'd go with anyone for a packet of chocolate," he said angrily.

"Ted, you know very well . . . " she said. She began to cry.

He was ready to go to work, in his hat and overcoat. He came to kiss her goodbye, though he was hurt. Her face was wet, and his heart burned.

He went off to his office. She went upstairs to her earrings. She put them on. They were lovely! Sweet! She looked in the mirror, smiling at herself. She was very happy, and very pretty, and she wore them all morning, in the house. She did not think about her husband. He would always be there. So she could have these little adventures. It was quite safe. She would always come home to him.

She had been a worker in Sam Adams' factory before her marriage. Adams was unmarried, about forty, well-dressed, solid. Everyone knew he liked the girls and they liked him. He liked Elsie. She was quick, a pretty quick little thing. But meanwhile Whiston wanted to marry her, and she knew he would always love her. So she felt free to play.

Every Christmas Sam Adams gave a party for his workers. Two years ago, Elsie went to this party with Whiston.

She was pleased with herself, in her blue silk dress with its full skirt. He carried her dancing shoes in his pocket.

The room was full of lights and music. Adams

came forward and welcomed them. Whiston didn't dance. So Elsie danced with Sam Adams.

He was an excellent dancer. The music carried them warmly, happily. When the dance was over she went to Whiston. He was not smiling.

"I do wish you could dance," she said.

"Well I can't," he said. "So enjoy yourself."

"But I'd enjoy it more, if I could dance with you. You ought to dance."

"It's all right," he said. "You enjoy yourself."

She danced again with Sam Adams' arms round her. There was a light in his eyes when he looked at her, and this pleased her. And she felt a little angry with Whiston.

Whiston went to another room to play cards. She danced with Adams again, and then again. The music carried them together round the room. They danced like one person. When the music stopped she felt unreal. She stood in the middle of the room with him and felt they were alone together. He bent over and kissed her shoulder. But they were not alone, they were not alone. It was cruel.

He took her to the supper-room. Whiston was there, taking coffee to the ladies who were not dancing. He came to her and she put her head on his shoulder. But he was uncomfortable. She was laughing and excited because of another man.

"Aren't you tired of dancing?" he said.

"Not a bit," she said.

"Not she," said Sam Adams in his loud voice. "Elsie, have some wine, have a glass of wine. Whiston, have a glass of wine with us."

They drank the wine and Adams watched Whiston.

"Listen," he said suddenly. "There's the music. Come, madam, the music is waiting for you. Whiston, take the ladies something to eat, will you?"

He began to move, back to the music, and Elsie went helplessly with him. Dancing, she forgot herself, only Adams was real, and his warmth seemed to melt into her.

When the dance was over he left her with Whiston in the supper room.

"Shall we go?" said Whiston. "It's nearly one o'clock. We've been here since nine."

"Must we go?"

"Haven't you had enough? Aren't you tired?"

She looked across the room at Sam Adams.

"You must be careful of Sam Adams," he said. "You know what he is."

She was silent.

Then she said, "I like him."

"Why?"

"I don't know – but I like him."

He sat with a heavy feeling of anger. He sat there, while she danced with Adams again. But she began to suffer. She breathed heavily, and she became anxious. Adams felt it. He too was angry. He could feel, beyond the girl in his arms a strong will, Whiston's will, which pulled her away from him. And she could feel Whiston like a heavy place in her heart.

She put her hand in her pocket, to take out her handkerchief. She shook it and it fell from her hand. It was not a handkerchief. She had put a white stocking in her pocket, instead of a handkerchief. For a second, it lay on the floor. Then Adams picked it up, with a little laugh.

59

"I'll take it," he whispered. "It's mine." He put it in his pocket, and offered her his own handkerchief.

When the dance was over and she was back with Whiston he said, "What did you drop?"

"I thought it was my handkerchief, but I'd taken a stocking by mistake," she said.

"And he's got it?"

"Yes."

"Why? What does he mean?"

She lifted her shoulders.

"Is he going to keep it?"

She did not answer.

"You'll let him keep it?"

He jumped up, full of black anger.

"No," she said, catching his arm. "No, Ted!"

"I won't stay here. Are you coming with me?"

She got up without a word and in a few moments they were in the street.

"What did you mean?" he said, still dark with anger. "That great pig," he added.

They went home in silence, through the cold empty darkness of the town. They were near her house, but she did not want to go inside.

"We'll walk on, into the fields," he said, and held her arm. She could not speak. He didn't understand her.

"What's the matter?"

She began to cry.

At last he took her into his arms. "Tell me what's the matter, Elsie, tell me my dear, tell me." He kissed her wet face.

"Ted," she whispered.

"What, my love?" he answered. He felt afraid.

"Be good to me," she said. "Don't be cruel to

me."

"No, no, pet," he said, surprised and unhappy. "Why?"

"Oh be good to me," she cried.

He held her very tight and his heart burned with love for her. His mind did not understand, but he loved her and believed in her. Then she was his again.

She refused to work at the factory again. Sam Adams did not try to persuade her.

In a few weeks, she and Whiston were married. She loved him deeply, she gave him a trust in himself. Nothing worried him now. Underneath everything, beneath all the things he did, was this completely sure love. This gave him freedom. They spoke about the white stocking once or twice. But he did nothing about it. "Ah, what does it matter?" he exclaimed.

Elsie was quite happy at first. Then slowly, she got used to him. He was the ground of her happiness, but she got used to him, as to the air she breathed. He, however, did not get used to her in the same way. In marriage, she too found freedom. She did not need to look after herself. Her husband must do that. She was free, she was free to do anything.

So when, after a few months, she met Sam Adams, she was not unkind to him. She was a young wife, she had a new and exciting knowledge of men, she knew Adams was in love with her, she knew he wanted her. She did not care for him, but she couldn't help playing with him. When St. Valentine's day came, a white stocking arrived, with a brooch, a little jewelled pin. Luckily Whiston did not see it. She did not worry about it. She kept it.

Now she had the pearl earrings. Whiston would see them. She thought, "I'll say my mother gave them to me, I'll say they were my grandmother's."

Whiston came home, tired and unhappy.

"What did you do with the white stocking?" he said, his voice strong and hard.

"I put it in a drawer – why?" she said lightly.

"Why are you keeping it?"

"Because I've got a pair now."

He was silent and sat smoking by the fire. She ran upstairs and put on the white stockings and went downstairs in them.

"Look," she said. "New stockings, they're lovely."

She picked up her skirt and turned her head, looking at her pretty legs.

"Put your skirt down and don't be a fool," he said.

She began to dance round the room, lifting her feet like a dancer on the stage.

"You little fool, stop it. And put those stockings on the fire."

"I shan't. They'll be useful."

"Put them on the fire."

"I shan't," she sang. "I shan't I shan't I shan't."

He almost hated her.

"You'd like Sam Adams to see you, wouldn't you."

"Yes, I would. He might give me some more," she said, a little afraid. But she would not put the stockings on the fire.

"If you speak to him I'll break your neck," he said.

"I'm not frightened of you," she said coldly. But she was, she was white round the mouth.

He wanted to kill her. He was so angry that he rose and went out of the house, and stood in the garden, unable to see or hear.

After a few minutes he came in again. She stood and watched him, like a child, with tightly closed lips and big angry eyes.

"You're not going to tell me what I can do and what I can't," she said.

"I'll tell you this," he said. "If you see or speak to Sam Adams I'll break your neck."

"You don't know everything," she said with a strange little laugh. "He sent me a brooch and a pair of pearl earrings."

"He what?"

"Sent me a brooch and a pair of pearl earrings."

He stood up and came towards her and hit her hard across the mouth.

She fell against the wall. Her mouth was bleeding. He wanted to destroy her, but he was ashamed and sick. He sat heavily in his chair. She began to cry silently.

"Where are they?" he said.

"Upstairs."

"Bring them down."

"I won't."

He went upstairs and found the brooch and the earrings. He looked round the room, and found a little box. He made a parcel, and addressed it to Sam Adams. Then he went out to post it.

When he came back she was still crying.

"You ought to go to bed," he said.

She did not answer.

He sat down. "I shall sleep down here," he said. "You go to bed."

In a few moments she lifted her wet face and looked at him with red unhappy eyes, like a helpless child. Suddenly a painful feeling went through him. He went to her and very gently took her in his arms.

Then as she lay against his shoulder, she said, "I didn't – I didn't mean . . ."

"My love, my little love," he said, in deep pain, holding her in his arms.